How the question, Who, Revolutionized marketing for me.
By- Rishi viz Krishna Mohan Avancha

Index

Table of Contents
5 Rings of Buying Insight for Buyer Personas......... 13
6 ways to inspire your buyer to take the plunge....36
17 Helpful Market Research Tools and Resources 45
    1) Think With Google: Marketer's Almanac.... 45
    2) American Fact Finder... 45
    3) County Business Patterns...............................45
    4) Business Dynamics Statistics........................45
    5) FedStats..46
    6) Nielsen MyBestSegments................................46
    7) SurveyMonkey... 46
    8) Typeform..47
    9) Survata... 47
    10) Loop11... 48
    11) Userlytics.. 48
    12) Temper...48
    13) MakeMyPersona... 49
    14) Ubersuggest.. 49
    15) Pew Research Center...................................... 49
    16) Social Mention.. 50
    17) HubSpot Research...50
    A great board of specialists................................. 72
18 Ways to Revive a Failed Product or Service....... 93

INTRODUCTION

Ever since I read the book, Start with Why? By Simon Sinek I have been left perplexed. I completely agree with what he had to say and yes I do have a very high regards for him for having shared such a wonderful thought and stating it out with such simplicity but I would still like to put it that I don't think that the question he put forward should be the only one but most definitely should be the first. I Think that post answering the question Why, every business owner must stop and ask the question, Who? Who do they think would most likely like or pay for their product or services. As business owners, we first need to stop and create Buyers persona and then think as to why we would like to sell our product or service to them. Yes! Nevertheless the question of why would always arrive here, we would need to ask ourselves as to why we would like to sell but if our who goes wrong then so will our why.

My this book is dedicated to this question and how this question changed the way I viewed and perceived what marketing was . This book details out the various consumer personas that any business owner selling an X product or service would meet and whether they would be willing to pay for that product or service.

Introduction to Marketing
and what it is not

Before we dwell into the vastness of Zero, let's first understand what we know about marketing and what actually marketing is and what it most definitely is not.

Marketing is most definitely the underlying sense in understanding the human needs, lets also for discussion sake dwell into the topic of what marketing most definitely is not.

1. Marketing isn't deals. We have a customer that views themselves as a promoting association, however the main thing they do is bolster deals. We've invested a great deal of energy instructing them on what it is that makes a showcasing association and what they're doing isn't it.

2. Advertising isn't hard. It's mind boggling. In any case, it's not hard. Discover individuals who your item or administration could help and give them data that causes them settle on a purchasing choice.

3. Marketing more often than not does not give everyday item support. With the assistance of different web based life groups, what showcasing can do is make valuable and drawing in post-item bolster content. To be executed well, advertising needs an item the board staff who have profound item mastery.

4. Promoting is in charge of making and supporting corporate idea administration. In any case, in spite of what some senior administrators might want you to think, showcasing is anything but an individual exposure machine concentrated on getting at least one officials in the general population spotlight. For these endeavors, administrators should enlist their very own attention operators.

5. Emergency the executives, particularly in the present all day, every day news cycle, frequently falls under the umbrella of continuous PR. Actually, when progressed nicely, emergency the executives needs to cross numerous corporate capacities including senior administration, client administration, lawful, HR, activities and financial specialist relations just as showcasing.

6. Advertising's capacity to elevate an organization to planned workers and to help HR correspondences are vital components inside the general interchanges work. In any case, HR is still at last in charge of these capacities.

7. For business-to-business advertising, couple of weapons prevail just as telemarketing. Telemarketing reaction can be enhanced by enlarging it with promoting. Be that as it may, don't mess with yourself. Advertising isn't telemarketing alone.

8. More cash has been squandered by expecting marvels than by some other misguided judgment of advertising. Promoting is the best speculation you can make whether you do it right, and doing it right requires tolerance and arranging.

While advertising drives and backings deals, it is generally another person's business to make it happen. Showcasing, at its center, is tied in with building up the methodologies and strategies that help accomplishing an association's objectives by building associations with prospects, clients and people in general. In any case, others ordinarily execute these methodologies and strategies.

Final words: Branding is dependably the core of your marketing endeavors since it characterizes your group of onlookers, edge, one of a kind moving focuses, and message. Marketing is something that can be affected by everything your organization is doing. A mix-up made by the Finance or operations division can affect your marketing, for instance.

Marketing is tied in with everything your organization does, however advertisers are the principal line of resistance. They are regularly given the acknowledgment for good marketing choices, however they are additionally the first to be accused when things turn out badly.

BUYER PERSONAS

A buyer persona is a semi-anecdotal portrayal of your optimal client dependent on statistical surveying and genuine information about your current clients.

While making your purchaser persona(s), consider including client socioeconomically, standards of conduct, inspirations, and objectives. The more point by point you are, the better.

Buyer personas give huge structure and knowledge to your organization. A point by point purchaser persona will enable you to figure out where to center your time, control item advancement, and consider arrangement over the association. Therefore, you will almost certainly draw in the most profitable guests, leads, and clients to your business.

What is a Buyer Persona?

Worked from the genuine expressions of genuine purchasers, a purchaser persona discloses to you what forthcoming clients are considering and doing as they gauge their choices to address an issue that your organization settle. Considerably more than a one-dimensional profile of the general population you have to impact, or a guide of their adventure, significant purchaser personas uncover bits of knowledge about your purchasers' choices - the particular demeanors, concerns and criteria that drive imminent clients to pick you, your rival or the present state of affairs.

A purchaser persona isn't just a depiction of your purchaser. As several our accomplices and clients can let you know, basically profiling your purchaser results in such a large number of personas and not almost enough showcasing direction.

Be that as it may, when you have experiences into what your purchasers consider working with you, including verbatim statements from individuals who have as of late settled on the choice to take care of a comparative issue, you have the learning you have to adjust your promoting choices - from situating and informing through substance advertising and deals enablement – with your purchaser's desires.

The ROI is this basic: When you realize how to enable purchasers to assess your methodology all alone terms, you construct an obligation of trust that contenders can't coordinate.

5 Rings of Buying Insight for Buyer Personas

Need Initiatives

What makes certain purchasers put resources into arrangements like yours, and what is distinctive about purchasers who are happy with the present state of affairs?

Tips and Examples

Try not to mistake Priority Initiatives for torment focuses that you basically figure out dependent on the abilities of your answer.

You need to comprehend the individual or hierarchical conditions that reason your purchasers to distribute their time, spending plan, or political cash-flow to determine the agony.

For instance, you could figure that the advertising official purchaser persona has torment in the region of promoting measurements and battle robotization. Be that as it may, a savvy purchaser persona would disclose to you which showcasing officials are most (and least) open to your advertising computerization arrangement and why.

Achievement Factors

What operational or individual outcomes does your purchaser persona hope to accomplish by obtaining this arrangement?

Tips and Examples

Achievement Factors take after advantages, yet this knowledge is unmistakably increasingly explicit and composed from the purchaser's viewpoint.

For instance, you may as of now accentuate your answer's effect on cost decrease, however a quick purchaser persona would recognize the classification and level of cost decrease that purchasers foresee.

Instances of individual results incorporate inspiring friends, enlarging the purchaser's range of authority, or expanding their capacity to control something about their condition.

Seen Barriers

What concerns cause your purchaser to trust that your answer or organization isn't their best alternative?

Tips and Examples

Hope to pick up bits of knowledge into item or organization explicit hindrances that are never again (or never were) truly right.

These observations frequently result from negative encounters with comparative arrangements, online co-operations, or direct criticism from companions.

Different hindrances identify with individual or business snags that keep your purchaser from putting resources into change. Precedents incorporate the requirement for business process change, picking up acknowledgment from end clients, or other politically-charged issues.

Purchaser's Journey

This knowledge uncovers insights regarding who and what impacts your purchaser as they assess their choices and select one.

Tips and Examples

To enable you to focus on the most powerful purchaser personas, this knowledge recognizes which personas have the most effect on the choice to keep on assessing your answer at each progression all the while. (Tip: the monetary purchaser or leader isn't as compelling as you think.)

To enable you to organize your showcasing ventures, you have to know which assets the purchaser trusts at each progression of their assessment for this choice. For instance, an advertising official would not depend on similar assets for choices about web conferencing and off-web page occasion arranging.

For influential informing and substance, the Buying Process understanding indicates the Decision Criteria, Success Factor, and additionally Perceived Barrier that has the most effect on the purchaser's decision at each progression.

Choice Criteria

Which parts of the contending items, administrations, arrangements or organization does your purchaser see as most basic, and what are their desires for each?

Tips and Examples

You will know which of your capacities has the most effect on your purchaser's decision to work with you. (Tip: this is probably not going to identify with what is freshest or generally one of a kind).

This knowledge advises informing and substance showcasing choices, clearing up both the purchaser's inquiries and the appropriate responses they need to hear.

For instance, if the purchaser needs an answer that is "anything but difficult to-utilize", the Decision Criteria Insight indicates which parts of the arrangement this persona hopes to be "anything but difficult to utilize" and how they figure out which arrangement is the least demanding.

How to develop Buyer Personas

Hubspot is an excellent source of marketing tools and so you could head directly to this: https://www.hubspot.com/make-my-persona
Or this: https://offers.hubspot.com/persona-templates
To either develop your own buyer persona from scratch or to get the template to do so. Some other sources include:
https://www.contentharmony.com/blog/customer-persona-tools/
And:
https://www.demandmetric.com/content/buyer-persona-template

Some very good examples of buyer profiles, I found on where on this blog: https://blog.alexa.com/10-buyer-persona-examples-help-create/

BRANDI TYLER

PROFILE	Narrow Feet
GENDER	Female
AGE	36
LOCATION	Los Angeles, CA
OCCUPATION	Receptionist; $38k

MOTIVATIONS
Brandi gets very emotional about shopping for shoes in retail stores because she rarely can find a pair that fits her narrow feet. Recently, she's turned to online shopping to avoid the hassle of shopping in stores. Brandi found Munro after Googling "narrow width shoes" and reading other reviews online about the company.

GOALS
- Needs an SS (4A) width shoe
- Would like to purchase several pairs to fit occasion, style, and color
- Hoping to find that she doesn't have to sacrifice style or options when searching by fit

FRUSTRATIONS
- Not being able to filter available shoes by width
- Getting far fewer options when she applies width filter
- No other recommended shoes when she's looking at a pair she particularly likes

"It's SO difficult to buy shoes that fit my feet."

REAL MUNRO CUSTOMERS

"My whole life has been a choice between fit and style - when I was younger, I went for style & my feet killed me. As an adult, I tried for fit & the styles were for 95 year olds. This shoe is the 1st time I could get both."

"I wear a 4A and I have struggled my entire life finding shoes narrow enough for my feet and more so in recent years. I stumbled onto this Munro brand sandal and was shocked to find it comes in up to a 4A width and it actually fit and is like wearing a glove! I now have two pairs in different colors."

"Love these slides so much I went out and bought two more pairs. I have very narrow feet and they fit perfectly. They're very stylish and I get compliments whenever I wear them."

Coffee Shop Marketing Persona

Sarah Student

"I need to be able to go somewhere to relax, re-focus, and get inspired without breaking the bank."

A DAY IN THE LIFE OF SARAH
- Early mornings, late nights describes her daily routines, so she lives on coffee
- She goes to school all day, studies at nights and works freelance jobs
- She has a cat that keeps her grounded with a sense of responsibility
- She's a carefree college student
- Her house is never in order, her fridge is empty and she's always buried in a book or her laptop
- She takes the train and Ubers everywhere

BACKGROUND
- 20 years old
- Single
- Lives in San Francisco, CA
- Full-Time Interior Design Student, Part Time Worker

FINANCES
- Household income of $30,000
- She's super conscious about what she spends her money on
- Prefers to use her credit / debit cards

ONLINE BEHAVIORS
- Facebook is her life-line
- Active on Twitter, Instagram, and Pinterest
- Looks for coupons and good deals on cool, new experiences or restaurants

WHAT SHE'S LOOKING FOR
- A place to de-compress after a hectic week
- A quiet place to study where she's not distracted by her messy room
- A good deal to make her feel better about purchases
- A sense of stability in her chaotic world
- Cool, new experiences or adventures

WHAT INFLUENCES HER
- Her friends and colleagues
- Magazines, blogs, articles, and design publications

BRAND AFFINITIES
- Starbucks, H&M, Forever21, American Eagle, Target

HOPES & DREAMS
- Become a reputable interior designer
- Travel the world
- Have the flexibility to be able to pick up and go as she pleases
- Not have to worry about finances

WORRIES & FEARS
- Not being able to pay her bills
- Getting stuck somewhere and not being able to travel
- Not having enough time with her cat
- Not being able to pay back her school debt

MAKE HER LIFE EASIER
- Funky atmosphere that's inviting and relaxing
- Deals and coupons
- Provide a job-board inside the coffee shop for freelance jobs
- Cozy seating with plenty of charging stations
- Order drinks to-go online or through an app
- Social media engagement incentives for discounts

What are the main questions to ask in marketing?

This is the season that the vast majority of us consider our future. When the ball drops in Times Square, we survey our own lives and what we'd like to enhance with snapshots of reflection and posing in excess of a couple of inquiries: How would i be able to spend less or spare more? Do I have to get in shape or include another expertise or gain proficiency with a dialect? On the expert front, it's likewise a period for some to finish yearly self-evaluation: What did you achieve? How did that contrast with your arrangement? Do you merit a raise? Did you do what's necessary to gain an advancement?

In any case, the most imperative inquiry you have to get some information about your weight, your financial balance or your activity title. The most imperative inquiry that each advertiser needs to ask when they look in the mirror is basic: "What actions am I taking to enable my deals to group?"

The job of the advertiser is evolving. At no other time in history has the advertiser had this much chance - sitting in the C-suite, controlling this much spending plan, directing the client experience and cooperating to characterize corporate advancement. In any case, with that open door comes duty - driving income from mindfulness entirely through the pipe to client maintenance and extension to share of wallet.

As the job of promoting and showcasing initiative develops, the obligations change, however the focal point of the office continues as before: encourage deals.

Assess Your Mar tech Stack

The "how" of how you help deals is debatable, however it likely begins with innovation. Advertisers need to make mindfulness, discover leads and sustain those leads until they're prepared to converse with a business rep or until the lead finishes their buy on the web or via telephone. Innovation can encourage target and break down every one of those means, however the test of choosing as well as can be expected be overwhelming.

Much has been expounded on the far reaching martech scene. Scott Brinker has recognized in excess of 5,000 organizations pondering the open doors in his yearly Market Technology Landscape. Nearly everybody trusts the blast of sellers isn't reasonable and is bound for solidification. A few, as Joe Stanhope at Forrester Research, propose the guide will at last meet with publicizing innovation (adtech), influencing several billions of dollars in promoting spend.

With truly a large number of decisions influencing billions of dollars, by what method would marketers be able to channel through a logo soup of choices to settle on choices that show an arrival on showcasing speculation and move the needle for their associations? Stanhope's associate at Forrester, Carlton Doty, as of late discharged an extraordinary structure that difficulties and engages advertisers to thoroughly consider the making of their tech stack.

I would propose that, with the majority of the phenomenal systems and thought administration on the point, the basic inquiry that every advertiser needs to ask themselves initially is, "By what means will this assistance deals in my association?" With lucidity on that principal reply, fabricating your tech stack winds up less demanding. It's simpler to comprehend where to contribute, and less demanding to clarify where you won't contribute.

Use AI To Deliver Personal Customer Experiences

It's anything but difficult to become involved with the publicity around man-made consciousness. Everybody from tech organizations to futurists to financial speculators and tech journalists are swooning over the clearly boundless use cases for AI that may in the end usher humankind into an ideal world where our requirements are foreseen and flawlessly satisfied.

There are some expansive desires being worked around AI, and I concur the innovation shows gigantic guarantee in numerous fields. I'm comparatively sure that AI can possibly drastically change and enhance showcasing, enabling organizations to convey exceptionally customized client encounters, which thus will expand consumer loyalty and dedication.

However, once more, the crucial inquiry in my psyche is the means by which this helps a business association and how it drives income for an association. The present promoting still requires a considerable lot of human-based reaction to increment focusing on precision. Artificial intelligence will make showcasing a lot more astute, both in forecast and responsiveness, helping advertisers all the more effectively decide buy purpose and anticipate when prospects are prepared to purchase, notwithstanding focusing in zones, for example, promoting. It can envision and mechanize an affair on your corporate site, quickening the client venture on the web and diminishing the measure of time it takes from a prospect's first inquiry to extreme buy.

Artificial intelligence will likewise add to significant upgrades in call examination. Since the last advance in the client venture frequently closes with a telephone call - particularly for greater expense things like protection, car or travel - it's important that organizations comprehend what's going on inside each call. Artificial intelligence driven call investigation uncovers information focuses that assistance advertisers enhance call focus execution, distinguish high-purpose guests by catchphrases and re-target non-changing over guests.

The majority of this is cool and somewhat frightening. The majority of this makes our occupations simpler and a lot harder. In any case, I'd propose that everything needs to add up to something past "being cool" and should be separated through that solitary most imperative inquiry we ask ourselves this year.

As an advertiser, I'm energized for everything the New Year will bring: the difficulties, the triumphs, the new capacities to more readily serve clients that promoting tech will keep on releasing. Be that as it may, the total of the parts needs to come full circle in something bigger - the capacity to encourage our partners. Presently is simply the ideal time to test with the major inquiry of what we're doing to help. At the point when the ball drops in

Times Square, don't fail by neglecting to answer the inquiry yourself.

Some of the daunting questions to be asked for great sales and profits are:

1. When and where is your objective market when they are most inspired by your item?

2. What impacts and spurs your objective market?

3. How does your objective market need to be locked in with and spoken with?

4. What are the triggers that make your objective market choose the time has come to enter the market and afterward purchase?

5. Is your limited time procedure focused at getting new clients, expanding deals with existing clients or pulling in clients from your opposition?

6. What limited time strategies are your clients/potential clients well on the way to see, see and be keen on?

7. What limited time techniques do your clients/potential clients lean toward/esteem?

8. What limited time strategies have worked the best/most exceedingly bad for you and why?

9. What limited time techniques have worked the best/most exceedingly terrible for your opposition and why?

10. Are there any limited time strategies utilized in different ventures that may be fruitful whenever utilized for your business?

11. What are limited time strategies that will set aside next to no opportunity to execute and are free or no expense?

12. Could your business profit by a PR battle or trick?

13. Is the informing you are utilizing in your special strategies predictable and bring out feelings and contemplations that tempt individuals to activity?

14. Would it be advantageous for you to contract somebody with advertising background to assist you with your special endeavors?

Product/Services

1. What contender items/administrations are right now the

best and for what reason would they say they are fruitful?

2. What contender items/administrations are right now the most disastrous and for what reason would they say they are the most disastrous?

3. What item/benefit needs are not at present being met?

4. What items/administrations do your clients right now esteem the most?

5. What highlights of every item or administration do your clients right now esteem the most?

6. In what capacity can your items/administrations be made strides?

7. How might you lessen the expense of your items or administrations without changing their apparent incentive with clients?

8. Okay have the capacity to make more cash by lessening the expense to deliver your item or benefit and encountering a relating decline in deals?

9. Which items/administrations of yours do your clients esteem the most?

10. What extra items/administrations do you have the ability to move that you as of now are not moving?

11. What capacities or highlights of your item/benefit make clients irritated?

12. What capacities or highlights of your rival's item make their clients irritated?

13. What highlights and advantages are clients searching for in your market?

14. What highlights and advantages do clients esteem the most?

15. What highlights and advantages, that are profoundly esteemed by forthcoming clients, would you be able to give superior to your opposition?

16. What is an issue that huge numbers of your clients have, that you can comprehend, and is an answer that you can pitch to them as an item or administration?

Price

1. On a size of one to ten, how imperative is cost for clients and prospects in your objective market?

2. What highlights and advantages are clients willing to pay more for?

3. What highlights and advantages are clients willing to pay almost no or nothing for?

4. What are the evaluating patterns that are as of now happening in your market?

5. What is the most minimal extraordinary value you at present offer?

6. What is a value that new clients can't cannot?

7. What is the lifetime benefit created from another client?

8. How does your evaluating contrast with the challenge?

9. What are ways that you can expand the cost gotten for your items/administrations?

10. Are there any advantages to changing your estimating terms, installment terms or contract length?

11. What estimating techniques of your rivals are working/not working?

12. Which of your evaluating techniques are working or not working?

13. What evaluating model is the best for your item or administration? (find out about estimating procedures)
14. Would you be able to build cost with negligible to no diminish in deals?

15. When you drop your cost, do your business spike fundamentally or remain generally level?

16. Would you be able to make more cash by raising or bringing down your normal value given the subsequent changes in volumes?

17. Would you be able to make more cash by raising or bringing down your element value given the subsequent changes in volumes?

18. At what cost does your item or administration give extraordinary incentive to your clients?

19. Place (ie. Conveyance Channels)

20. Where does your objective market make buys and are your items sold there?

21. Do you have a solid nearness where your objective market makes buys for the items and administrations you move?

22. How does your objective market need to be locked in with and how would they like to purchase?

23. What are all the circulation techniques utilized by your opposition to move its items?

24. What are all the circulation techniques utilized by the best organizations in your industry?

25. What are all the dispersion strategies utilized by your organization to move its items?

26. Are there extra dissemination strategies you could use to move your items where you could contend viably?

27. Is there in any case you could make your present appropriation framework increasingly proficient or successful?

28. What baffles your clients as of now about the obtaining procedure for your items?

29. Would your business have the capacity to profit by an organization, joint endeavor, permitting assertion or moving establishments?

6 ways to inspire your buyer to take the plunge

Do you know why your clients are purchasing from you? Is it your items—the style and nature of your high quality work? Look further and you will find that there are numerous different factors in making a deal that you can use in building your business volume.

Its an obvious fact that feelings are incredible elements that move individuals without hesitation and cause them to make a buy. To build your business, you should comprehend and speak to them inwardly. There are numerous different craftsmen and craftspeople out there with magnificent contributions.

For what reason will that client pick you?

1. Make them feel exceptionally unique. Grin and genuinely welcome your client. Trade pleasantries without heading off to a hard move first. Your demeanor must be one of neighborly administration and enthusiasm for them.

2. Offer heaps of data. Buyers search for reliable, proficient people to instruct them on a buy. Trust is the most vital factor prompting long haul connections and rehash deals.

3. Clients should be associated with the choice. Help them by utilizing tangible systems. In the event that conceivable, put

the article being considered in their grasp. This offers contact, as well as a feeling of proprietorship, which you ought to empower. State, "Your new hoops will look awesome with that equip." Encourage customers to contact a texture, handle and tune in to your high quality instruments, taste or smell the items if suitable.

4. Tell your story. How could you imagine this new procedure of working? Did an excursion to a remote nation rouse you? Where did you run over a magnificent antique texture utilized in your creation? Stories are a ground-breaking connector which will turn out to be "a piece of your item," and the purchaser will retell those accounts when demonstrating their buy to other people.

5. Make acceptable vows. Taking an uncommon request for a client? Speak the truth about the time period and ensure you development. Get in touch with them after the request to express gratitude toward them once more, and console them about their request, however don't over-guarantee. Be practical, and after that surpass their desires!

6. Provide a high level of service.. Show regard for them and for their time by being on schedule for any arrangements you may have set up. On the off chance that you are

late, call. Be steady with a brisk reaction, and keep them very much educated.

7. Invite them to tell their story. However drastic it may sound, every customer wants to talk and they talk too while making a purchase from you. Make them feel that their voice is heard by listening to them and recording to reciprocate the same with some kind of a physical act. Imagine a customer says that his son is too naughty and keeps bumping into things, kids are known to do such things. This is the perfect opportunity which you can use and probably during your first year party could present the customer with Baby Security Anti-crash Protector With Tape - Believe me the customer will never forget this simple gift as it proves that you were hearing them and share their pain with them unlike others who did nothing to make them feel special.

These procedures lead to building trust, which obviously is the reason your clients will keep on purchasing from you and allude others to you. They anticipate an incentive in your items, and they likewise need to feel esteemed. This is also proving to your customers that they matter to you and you are ready to go the extra mile just to make them feel special. Understanding why your clients are truly purchasing from you will empower you to develop deals volume and make durable beneficial connections.

Has Marketing Lost its Value?

Marketing can probably never lose its value but it can surely loose relevance with the customer expecting something more customized for each of their need. Mass marketing is no longer a trend which is appreciated. Take for example those countless emails that you get on a daily basis via gmail that you calmly mark as spam as they may not have your name correct or maybe the writer did not get an accurate background of the receiver.

P&G just cut $140 million in ad spend, Coke fired its CMO and the current ad blocking trend is possibly the largest consumer boycott in history at 600 million devices and growing. All this as most marketers have most conveniently ignored the pleas of customers to ensure relevance to them in the ads or emails or telephone calls.

In today's busy world even the customer wants to be associated with brands who keep their data safe and remember them forever from their likes to their choices. Take for example Apple or Starbucks who always refer to you with your correct email and other details just to either wish you or update you on a new product that you may be interested in based on your choices made the last time you visited them. These days you will find similar techniques being used by Ajio, a brand of reliance who are taking personalization and relevance to a new level with customized SMS, emails and offers based on the customers choice of purchases.

The old idea that marketing is about advertising, branding and pushing messages is flawed. A quick comparison of Tesla and Daimler-Benz shows this to be true. Mercedes C-Class sold 77,000 cars in 2016 in the United States. Tesla, targeting the same market, sold 325K. Mercedes spent 90 times more than Tesla on advertising their product, and sold one-fourth of the volume sales of Tesla. The key difference is not in how they advertised but in how they viewed marketing.

Tesla follows a primary marketing business model which is to market first to create a connect with their audience, sell second and build third. It sold three times as many cars with this model and without its cars even existing. Mercedes still follows the old business model where marketing is a secondary function designed to sell the products it has developed and is represented by the build first, market second and sell third model where quintessentially marketing always comes second base only to support sales and not build a brand or connect with the audience.

17 Free Tools that can help you better understand your target audience

17 Helpful Market Research Tools and Resources

1) Think With Google: Marketer's Almanac

Value: Free

Wish you had data on how purchaser conduct changes in connection to the seasons, occasions, and other exceptional occasions? Think With Google's Marketer's Almanac offers fascinating bits of knowledge on how individuals peruse and purchase.

2) American Fact Finder

Value: Free

American Fact Finder is an asset for looking U.S. statistics information. You can channel by age, pay, year, race, and area.

3) County Business Patterns

Value: Free

District Business Patterns gives data on the zones of the nation with huge quantities of specific sorts of organizations.

4) Business Dynamics Statistics

Value: Free

Business Dynamics Statistics takes registration information and permits you see monetary information on employment creation, new companies and shutdowns, business openings, extensions, and terminations.

business-elements

5) FedStats

Value: Free

FedStats gives a forward-thinking gathering for discovering information discharged by government offices, including agribusiness, instruction, transportation, and vitality.

6) Nielsen MyBestSegments

Value: Free

Nielsen's MyBestSegments gives specialists devices to comprehend a region's statistic data and way of life propensities. You can discover which regions would be most responsive to a crusade or dispatch, which contenders are found close-by, and drifts in the territory that have moved.

7) SurveyMonkey

Value: Free for Basic, $26/month for Select, $25/month for Gold, $85/month (per client) for Platinum

SurveyMonkey is a useful asset for making inside and out studies that will enable you to comprehend the market and buyer inclinations. (Get familiar with making an overview for statistical surveying here.)

8) Typeform

Value: Free for Basic, $35/month for Pro, $70/month for Pro+

Typeform demonstrates watchers one structure field at once, and you can incorporate various decision picture choices. It's a simple to-utilize, versatile streamlined structure developer that is incredible for social occasion criticism.

9) Survata

Cost: $1/respondent for Basic, $2.50/respondent for Extended

Survata is another structure building alternative, yet you can decide an intended interest group. It likewise utilizes individuals who will audit your review questions, so regardless of whether you are not a prepared economic scientist, you can get quality, noteworthy answers.

10) Loop11

Cost: $158/month for Micro, $410/month for SMB, $825/month for Enterprise

Loop11 is an ease of use testing administration that enables you to test even your rivals' sites - any site page, fundamentally. You can make a structure and enlist individuals to step through the examination through your own site or by utilizing an accomplice administration, for example, Cint.

11) Userlytics

Value: Variable (begins at $2,900/year for one session)

Userlytics gives a stage to doing client testing of portable applications, recordings, show advertisements, and that's only the tip of the iceberg. It performs both a webcam and a screen recording, and you can contrast the client answers and their responses on record to see how individuals are truly connecting with your innovative.

12) Temper

Cost: $12/month for Hobby, $49/month for Pro, $89/month for Business, $199/month for White Label

Here and there you need a straightforward test to take the beat of purchasers. Temper enables you to include an inquiry, snatch a piece of code, and pop it onto your site. The smiley face, "meh" face, and glare face make it simple for watchers to make a snap judgment.

13) MakeMyPersona

Value: Free

The MakeMyPersona apparatus is an intelligent web instrument that produces purchaser personas for you once you answer a progression of inquiries concerning your optimal clients. The apparatus gives a lot of direction all through the procedure, making it extremely simple for you to deal with the data you have about your optimal group of onlookers.

14) Ubersuggest

Value: Free

Ubersuggest is a basic apparatus for doing catchphrase and substance explore. You can include an expression, and it'll release a since quite a while ago, ordered rundown of extra watchwords.

15) Pew Research Center

Value: Free

From financial conditions, to political frames of mind, to online life use, the Pew Research Center site has a huge amount of free research that you can use to all the more likely comprehend your objective market. The best part is that the site has a smooth UI and intelligent outlines that uncover increasingly granular information as you drift over specific components.

16) Social Mention

Value: Free

Social Mention is a continuous internet based life web crawler that can enable you to comprehend what your planned clients are humming about on the web. Scan for a catchphrase, and Social Mention will indicate you late social posts that contain that watchword, alongside a rundown of related watchwords and different bits of knowledge.

17) HubSpot Research

Value: Free

Need to perceive how site traffic changes by industry, or how powerful publicizing is in various districts the world over? HubSpot Research has got you secured. Notwithstanding looking at our free research reports, you can utilize HubSpot Research's introduction manufacturer device to effectively accumulate details and graphs into a tweaked slide deck.

13 Key Strategies For Building A Successful Brand In Today's Economy

A brand is far beyond a logo or its visual components, and building a solid one is frequently equivalent to, if not progressively imperative, than the item or administration itself.

A swarmed market, not understanding your objective TGT - 1.36% client, freshness — these components may influence your capacity to be fruitful, particularly as a first-time entrepreneur. It's anything but difficult to escape with overcomplicated systems, however keep your sights on the center components with regards to making your image. Beneath, individuals from Forbes Coaches Council clarify what these are:

1. Influence The Testimonial Economy

We presently live in the tribute economy. We never again tune in to what others state about themselves. Rather, we go online to realize what individuals state about them. Impacted by their remarks, we settle on a progressively educated purchasing choice. Need to construct an effective brand? Influence the tribute economy by building a network of represetatives prepared to share their affection for your image on the web.

2. Make Emotive Appeal

A key method to fabricate a fruitful brand is to utilize emotive intrigue by making a relationship between the item or administration and a feeling. When we comprehend the key wants and battles of our objective market, we can assemble a brand persona that demonstrates how our item can enable our objective to showcase accomplish their ideal condition of feeling. Most purchasing choices are passionate in nature.

3. Concentrate On Generating Value For Others

Individuals infrequently recall what you said or did, however they recollect how you affected them. Trust is the most imperative cash in the 21st century, and the individual you're serving must feel the validity of your character and experience your capability direct. Create an incentive for others multiple times previously requesting anything consequently. In the event that your administration is special, your image will be cemented.

4. Utilize The Internal Dialog Of Your Clients

Talk your prospects' language. We will in general use advertising words to characterize our image. What is your prospect saying to their accomplice over the supper table? Are they utilizing words like "arrangement, coordinated effort or commitment?" More likely they are stating, "We can't complete things, nobody minds that we are behind, we are missing due dates, once more." Use what they state in your marking materials.

5. Be Known For A Specific Niche

Try not to sloppy your message by telling prospects you are a specialist in different things. For instance, saying you are a picture advisor for people is a significantly less amazing message than saying you are a picture expert gaining practical experience in ladies more than 40 who are reappearing the workforce subsequent to being housewives. Being explicit enables you to be vital and the best in your specialty.

6. Recognize And Target Your Ideal Client

To have a solid brand you have to know, see and bid to your key statistic. The most ideal approach to do this is to make your optimal customer symbol in crystalline detail. Think about geology, age, parental status, most loved television programs, objectives, online status, instruction level, feelings of trepidation, dreams, shortcomings, loathes, and so on. When you know who this individual is, you can move informing to talk specifically to this individual.

7. Be Consistent

A brand is a guarantee of an affair and is straightforwardly associated with trust. On the off chance that you need to construct a fruitful brand, first be sure about the brand identity. What are the ABC's: properties, practices and qualities of the brand? At that point guarantee that each connection a customer has with the brand imbues those ABC's into it. Consistency assembles trust and cements the brand.

8. Comprehend Branding Is Not About Positioning

Drop the conviction that marking is tied in with situating. Your image is the entirety of how individuals experience you. Experience goes past visual character and showcasing messages. Truly, dial in your informing, yet additionally search for approaches to wow individuals in their experiences with you. See each touch point as a chance to inspire your clients and abandon them resting easy thinking about themselves, not simply your image.

9. Discover The Intersection

An effective brand is the convergence between what you want to do, what you are astounding at, and what others need and need. On the off chance that you adore what you do yet others needn't bother with it, at that point it's a side interest. To fabricate a brand, your endowments must reverberate profoundly and satisfy a requirement for your gathering of people. Do this reliably after some time and your image will end up effective.

10. Offer Your Brand Assets In A Thought Leadership Campaign

You used to require a blog so as to showcase your image effectively, yet nowadays LinkedIn, LNKD +0% makes that simple by means of their long-structure post highlight. By utilizing this element, talk posts, and announcements, you can delicately advance your image resources without giving off an impression of being showcasing yourself by any stretch of the imagination. Concentrate on sharing really accommodating substance, experience and astuteness to draw in your optimal market.

11. Be Authentic

Try not to attempt to be something you are most certainly not. Others see through that — and it smothers your certainty. Be your identity (the great and the awful) so you will pull in other people who "get" you. That is who you need in your clan. Ensure your online visual portrayal matches who individuals see when they meet you face to face. It features your trust in yourself, your aptitudes, and demonstrates your validness.

12. Watch What Makes Your Heart Pound

When you tell others what you do, or share your best with a customer or prospect, what makes your heart pound? What gets your juices streaming? What do you end up saying again and again, in light of the fact that it's so key to your identity and how you (and your organization) serve the world? That is your message. Furthermore, that is the focal point for what will end up being your image. It's you. Begin there.

13. Characterize Your Brand's DNA

DNA is characterized as "major and particular attributes/characteristics of something" and "unchangeable." If your group can't rapidly shake off your image's DNA by heart, put pen to paper, Create a rundown of benchmark brands from an optimistic viewpoint and discover normal subjects. Distinguish key characteristics that epitomize your image. Regardless of whether it's value leverage or specialty, characterize it's center and remain consistent with it.

64 Creative Marketing Ideas to Boost Your Business

We've all hit it – that divider that appears to sap away the entirety of your otherworldly inventive promoting juices. All of a sudden you feel like Peter Pan without his pixie dust.

64 Creative Marketing Ideas to Boost Your Business

All you need is a touch of assistance to kick your promoting technique in the groove again. What's more, prepare to have your mind blown. We're dishin' out 64 imaginative promoting and publicizing thoughts in addition to rousing tips to enable you to bust through that block divider, create more leads and increment online deals. How about we begin with...

Internet based life Marketing Ideas

Urban Marketing Ideas

Challenge Marketing Ideas

Showcasing Ideas for Contest Promotion

Content Marketing Ideas

Internet based life Marketing Ideas

Push your handles – If you're truly hoping to knock up those Twitter devotees, you can't be hesitant to be somewhat bold. Talking at a meeting? Put your Twitter handle on the slideshow (hell, keep it in the corner the whole introduction). Requesting new business cards? Better incorporate that delightful handle!

twitter promoting

Extremely cool Twitter-themed business card from Luis Felipe Silva

Participate on week after week hashtag topics like #ThrowbackThursday – If you need to construct your web-based social networking following, you should be a functioning member in the network. This implies posting routinely, and furthermore participate on fun week by week internet based life customs that as of now have a devoted gathering of people. Demonstrate the children how hip you can be!

Vines – Vines, speedy 6-second video cuts, are to a great extent under-used. With a little work and some fun substance, you could turn into a major fish in a little lake on Vine.

vine advertising

Stick your very own pictures (and others) - Don't belittle the estimation of this picture sharing site. Post your most grounded visual resources (formats, info graphics, and so forth) on Pinterest and connection them to your website pages for some genuine traffic.

Keep social tabs on contenders - Facebook business pages enable you to pursue different records through the Pages to Watch include. Pursue your rivals and see what they post, and which of their posts get the most offers and likes. See what works and pursue their lead.

facebook pages to observe

From Inside Facebook

Urban Marketing Ideas

Living in a solid wilderness takes into consideration some entirely imaginative ideas.

Venture out in the city – In an online age, there's undeniable value in going natural and practicing a little IRL promoting. Run old fashioned with flyers and notice in nearby bistros, do some walkway chalk composing. This technique is best for privately situated organizations, yet it can work for anybody.

Road craftsmanship promoting

Road chalk Twitter handle by Marquette ITS

Commission a wall painting – Try motivating authorization to enhance the side of an unmistakable working with an expansive wall painting.

promoting wall painting

Extraordinary Di Bruno Bros wall painting found on Yelp

Utilize your environment – Get somewhat inventive and consider how you can utilize your urban surroundings for potential showcasing enchantment.

road advertising thoughts

Creative urban advertising endeavors by Vijar Barbecues, found on Owni

Irregular sponsorships – Urban living outcomes in some special advertising openings you won't discover somewhere else. They mystery is, you have to think inventively to benefit from these chances.

urban showcasing thoughts

Citi Bank supporting Citi Bike (picture from Bicycling)

Reward: We've pulled these tips (and included 5 more!) into a PDF for you to peruse later. Download it here - >

Challenge Marketing Ideas

Photograph Contests - Photo challenges are incredible for a number for reasons – they're moderately simple to enter (anybody with Instagram and a couple of extra seconds can submit), and they likewise give supports an extraordinary type of client produced substance that can be reused and actualized somewhere else.

Look at Harpoon Brewery – they've aced the craft of photograph challenges. (Also, click here for more Instagram advertising thoughts.)

internet based life advertising thoughts

Video challenges - Not the same number of individuals will participate in video challenges, yet you're bound to get a higher gauge of substance since making a video requires more exertion on the client's part. This sort of substance can be very important for organizations down the line, particularly when you have skilled filmers making video content only for you!

Present your vote challenges - Voting challenges get a huge amount of passages since they're so natural to partake in (simply click a catch, as a rule). What's cool about casting a ballot challenges is that you can utilize the information got from the votes to make a smaller than usual information ponder. Offer what you realized in a blog entry!

Subtitle Contests - Post a photograph and request that clients present their best inscription - this sort of challenge can get some really incredible snickers.

subtitle challenge

Sweepstakes - The most customary of challenges, sweepstakes/giveaways are an attempted and genuine great. They are brisk and easy to enter – in addition to it's anything but difficult to request email memberships as a feature of the accommodation structure.

Advertising Ideas for Contest Promotion

Post to bargain destinations - People love free stuff, some more than others. The general population who truly love a decent arrangement will in general successive arrangement destinations and discussions. There's quite often a sweepstake/challenge discussion segment where you can include your challenge in with the general mish-mash.

I've seen challenges in which 90% of traffic is driven from these kinds of locales – okay, they aren't generally the most qualified leads, yet on the off chance that you need amount over quality, this is a sound methodology. Beginning of submitting to Slickdeals and go from that point. This can be an extraordinary type of eatery advertising.

Hashtag-ify your challenge - Adding an applicable (and novel) hashtag to your challenge encourages you monitor sections and makes them simple to look over and sort out. Moreover, they're out and out fun.

Make challenges very sharable - This implies including "share this challenge" catches on the off chance that you have a passage structure on a site, or essentially reassuring social partaking when all is said in done. The more individuals who think about your challenge, the merrier (for you at any rate)! Need more thoughts for Facebook? Download our free guide here!

challenge advancement thoughts

Offer extra focuses for sharing - If you offer clients extra focuses for sharing news of your challenge through online life, they'll be substantially more prone to surrender. Devices like Rafflecopter make it simple to offer clients additional sections for various activities (for example Joining the mailing list = +5 passages. Sharing challenge on Twitter = +2 passages).

challenge promoting thoughts

(picture from Website Spot)

Tell email endorsers of challenge - Remember, you definitely realize that your email supporters like you and are keen on what you bring to the table. In case you're running a challenge for a free year of your product, you realize your endorsers are going to need access!

Advance your challenge on (every single) social medium - If you're running a photograph challenge by means of Instagram, ensure despite everything you advance the challenge on Facebook, Twitter, Pinterest, and so on. You need every one of your supporters, over every single social medium systems to think about your incredible giveaway!

social showcasing thoughts

Offer catches from Wordpress module

Download our free manual for 10 Smart and Easy Facebook Marketing Ideas!

Content Marketing Ideas

Compose for your group of onlookers – The best bits of substance are the ones coordinated at your key crowds. Comprehend your client: realize their agony focuses, what gets them psyched, and what keeps them up during the evening. Executioner content location your gathering of people's needs and concerns!

Add a visual component to ALL your substance pieces – People get exhausted with content truly quick! To keep guests perusing, it's basic to have pictures separating your content sections. Try not to ignore the significance of a visual component, even in blog entries that are dominatingly message based. You can see a few instances of exceptionally visual business writes here.

Infographics – We realize perusers love visual substance, and infographics are a prime case of darling, linkable visual resources.

content advertising thoughts

While making a first rate infographic may sound overwhelming, it doesn't need to be hard. You needn't bother with extravagant programming – truth be told, you can make a not too bad infographic simply utilizing Powerpoint. There are a lot of infographic guides layouts out there to kick you off. Talking about...

Valuable formats - Templates are another incredible type of visual resources that guests find very supportive. Formats fill in as a visual system that can enable clients to make custom piece without totally beginning starting with no outside help. Take this greeting page format for instance – it clarifies the fundamental design and basics, giving clients a chance to get a grip on incredible point of arrival basics before making their own.

showcasing thoughts for private ventures

Diagrams and Charts - The infographic's less cool cousins, one-piece diagrams outlines still have their place as imposing bits of visual substance. They may not be as amazing as infographics, yet they require significantly less time and exertion to make are as yet shareable, so don't be reluctant to utilize them liberally. For visual students, a diagram will be a lot less demanding to translate than a lump of content and numbers. Ensure you advance to a wide range of students!

showcasing graphs

That is the reason you find such a significant number of mythical serpents at the creature cover (picture from Reddit)

Recordings – Video is extraordinary with regards to attracting and holding the consideration of clients – consistency standard for visual data can achieve 65% versus 10% for content based data. Besides, clients who see item recordings are significantly more liable to change over than those that don't. Video content is an incredible asset, regardless of whether you're attempting to show how your item functions IRL or teaching guests.

Measurement records – Are you hitting a substance thought divider? For a simple substance promoting fix, gather fascinating insights on a topic identified with your business and make a blog entry about what you've realized. Monstrous detail records are anything but difficult to make and amazingly sharable. Furthermore, a portion of the more out of control details may get your riggings turning about other substance thoughts, for example,

Future forecasts – Play the seer by anticipating future patterns in your industry – simply ensure you have probably a few information to back up your theory.

Debate – Controversial substance dependably procures consideration, yet it's not for the black out of heart – behaving recklessly can get you consumed! As opposed to working up debate yourself, the more secure street might be to answer or react to bigger industry discussion with your own understanding.

disputable promoting thoughts

Gossipy tidbits travel quick

Total wonder from different sources - Another simple method to make executioner content is to minister quality substance from somewhere else. No, it's not taking ... at any rate, not whenever done appropriately.

It's totally genuine to acquire content from different sources in case you're exploring new territory with it. For instance, take our manual for the best SEO Reddit AMAs. The substance we cited from was initially posted on different Reddit discussion strings. We took what we regarded the "best" segments of the Q&As from various strings and set up everything together to make a super SEO counsel manage. This new post is a lot less demanding for clients keen on SEO to peruse, as opposed to scouring through different Reddit strings. NOTE: Play it safe by continually giving credit where it's expected.

Ask the specialists – Another incredible substance advertising thought is to talk with industry thought pioneers with set inquiries and offer their reactions in a blog entry; for instance, our meeting with industry specialists on the fate of PageRank. This sort of substance will in general progress nicely, and it's continually fascinating to see where industry masters concur and where they don't. One extraordinary thing about imparting master insights – odds are, the people you expound on will share your review with their own supporters! (Professional tip – solicit the suppositions from gatherings with substantial Twitter devotees!)

incredible promoting thoughts

A great board of specialists

Top 10s – People go crazy over best 10 records – top 10 devices, top 10 sites, and so on.

Records – Piggy-sponsorship on top 10s are records as a rule. Beginning your title with a number can make it emerge more in inquiry postings (for example 3 Ways to Slice a Pineapple). For what reason do individuals love records? Since they are excessively searchable and snappy to peruse. This is presumably why over 33% of Buzzfeed's posts have a number in the title. Extraordinary substance procedures include a blend of fast, snackable substance pieces and more inside and out, long-structure articles. Too much of the same thing will drive a person crazy.

Item correlation control – Decisions, choices – goodness, the traps of free enterprise. It's intense being a customer with such a significant number of items to browse. Help out clients with a showcasing examination direct, particularly on the off chance that you have a progression of item contributions for various requirements. In case you're contrasting your item and rivals, be target and reasonable; possibly you're a superior fit for private ventures, while a contender is better for bigger companies.

great advertising thoughts

Then again, review a correlation control for an item you don't offer, however which identifies with your crowd's matter of fact. For instance, a computer game affiliate could compose an item examination manage for various computer game controllers. This is useful substance that gets applicable clients comfortable with your image.

Content is an open entryway – Don't simply make amazing substance and relinquish it – highlight your best stuff in other related blog entries too. You can connection to or get out different bits of substance mid-post, or show some related articles toward the finish of your post. Something along the lines of "Need to become familiar with _____? Look at our _____ manage and our _____ infographic."

promoting thoughts

Content, love = apples, oranges. (Picture from Disney's Frozen)

Slideshare – The slideshow is back and over and above anyone's expectations! Repurpose PowerPoint introductions for crowd inviting slideshares. Look at these tips from Jonathan Colman on getting more perspectives on Slideshare.

Online classes – Host your own free online class or join forces with another business for double the aptitude (and double the advancement control). Online class are an incredible wellspring of business leads.

Google related hunt – Checking out the Google related ventures (found at the best and base of the SERP when you play out a pursuit) for a catchphrase inquiry is an incredible apparatus for creating content thoughts. Simply Google a term and see what related quests turn up. You might be amazed!

discover promoting thoughts

Spring up pick in – There's a ton of discussion around bulletin select in pop-ups. They're irritating, they're nosy, yet regularly, they additionally work! A/B test one and perceive how it influences your bulletin memberships. On the off chance that bulletin endorsers have turned out to be profitable leads for your business, do what you should to acquire them.

Proceed with your fortunate streak – Not certain what to expound on? Go into your investigation record and take a look at your most prominent presents on observe what subjects clients get amped up for, at that point compose a variety or expansion of a standout amongst your most famous posts.

digital books – Another incredible advertising thought is to compose a far reaching digital book on a realized torment point or well known industry theme, at that point make a quality greeting page around the offer. Even better, don't begin starting with no outside help; repurpose past blog entries and articles into a super digital book accumulation.

101 aides – There's dependably somebody simply beginning in the business; tenderfoot's aides and Industry Knowledge 101 substance pieces will dependably get connected to and shared around by newbs.

Indeed, even extraordinary substance needs advancement – Don't simply distribute your substance and anticipate that it should advance itself; share it with your email endorsers and internet based life supporters.

Post about industry intriguing issues – What's the buzz in your field? Post about topical news and inclining themes identified with your industry to get in on the burst of activity and demonstrate that you're up to date.

Visitor Posts – While the SEO estimation of visitor posts has been raised doubt about, there's nothing amiss with visitor posting whenever done right. Simply center around the estimation of getting your image before another group of onlookers, instead of the connections.

promoting thoughts

(Picture from Flickr client matsuyuki)

White papers – Guides, e-ooks, white papers – they're somewhat all a similar thing, yet marking your benefits diversely can enable your message to reverberate with various groups of onlookers. Test your names to see which works best with your prospects.

Quality substance – This ought to abandon saying, yet just produce quality substance that you can be pleased with! Google despises dainty substance, and clients don't care for it either.

Demonstrate some skin – I mean figurative skin obviously – demonstrate that you are not a robot. Try not to be reluctant to have some good times and hotshot your organization's identity. Convey what needs be; and in the event that that implies actually demonstrating some skin, well at that point, good luck with that. You're human all things considered.

great promoting thoughts

Online magazine – Producing your own virtual magazine is another epic type of substance advertising. For an extraordinary model, look at Dark Rye, an in vogue online magazine created by Whole Foods. For a snappy and simple fix, make your own online paper with Paper.li.

innovative showcasing thoughts

Webcasts – Podcasts are incredible in light of the fact that clients can download them and afterward tune in a hurry! Conceivable webcast ideas incorporate talking about hot industry news or meeting specialists, in your space.

Spread occasions – If you go to a meeting (or even an online occasion), consider composing a post about what data you accumulated from the occasion, what you discovered profitable, and so on. Odds are others will think that its profitable as well! Utilize the hashtag from the occasion in your special endeavors.

Joint effort – Collaboration can expand your scope and manufacture your notoriety. Consider all the distinctive associations you could manufacture – join forces with a philanthropy? A related business? You can co-creator a blog entry or guide, co-have an online class, and so forth.

Need to spare this rundown for some other time? We've made a helpful PDF for you (in addition to we included 5 progressively elite tips) - >

Images – Memes are fun and well-known for web goers. Get somewhat brazen with some fun images – it's anything but difficult to make your own with destinations like image generator.

super advertising thoughts

#SummertimeSadness

Social evidence – Sometimes extraordinary substance promoting thoughts likewise fill in as fabulous types of social confirmation. Take this creative substance venture by a spooky house called Nightmares Fear Factory. They take photographs of exploited people... er, I mean visitors, and post them to their Flickr feed. The photographs are totally insane and demonstrate that Nightmares Fear Factory is as unnerving as they guarantee to be! (Much obliged for the heads up from Shopify).

surprising promoting thoughts

Divvy up your substance – Don't go content-over the edge or you'll finish up overpowering clients. We live in an aggressive consideration economy, and in case you're making new stuff each and every day, individuals may feel sick of you, regardless of whether all that you share is brilliant. Them's the breaks, kid. Make sense of what pace works for your gathering of people.

Lead a content review – Is your current substance acceptable? What is driving transformations? What isn't – and why? Making these inquiries may make you sweat, however you'll be in an ideal situation knowing reality. Finding the responses to these inquiries will guarantee that your showcasing procedure pushes ahead the correct way.

Branded Tools – Create amazing, important apparatuses that your gathering of people will discover valuable. You can utilize parts of the apparatus to push towards your item offering, however ensure the instrument itself is high-gauge – don't simply make it a celebrated attempt to sell something. Giving free apparatuses will make clients consider affectionately you and expand your image as more individuals share your great free device!

Versatile! – With 79% of web clients directing web based shopping by means of cell phones, you ought to be humiliated in case you're not versatile benevolent. This isn't discretionary, albeit many still treat it as is it.

Gameification – Gamification is an incredible showcasing thought to get clients amped up for drawing in with you. As on Whose Line is it Anyway, the focuses are aimless, however you'd be astonished how much individuals truly appreciate getting focuses. We as a whole love moment confirmation – it resembles virtual split!

Applications like Belly and Foursquare consolidate gamification with client unwaveringness programs. Starbucks likewise has its very own manageable rendition of gamified steadfastness programs in which you acquire stars for Starbucks buys. Consider if gamification could work for your business.

dedication programs

Get by with some substance assistance from your companions – There are a huge amount of extraordinary devices out there to enable you to discover quality substance (Storify and Buffer to give some examples). Keep in mind, you would prefer not to simply share your own substance – sharing incredible pieces by others in your industry demonstrates that you're a cooperative person and significant wellspring of fair-minded information.

Funnies – While paper funnies are a diminishing breed, online funnies are alive and flourishing! Consider making your very own web funnies that identify with the foolish and dreamlike parts of your industry. Attempt free instruments like Pixton or Strip Generator to begin.

one of a kind advertising thoughts

Duplicate the bosses – Watch to see who is making extraordinary substance, and pursue their lead. Investigate misleading content destinations like Upworthy and Buzzfeed that get a huge amount of offers; while their gathering of people and substance subjects will be not the same as yours, they fill in as an astounding examination in how to enhance your advertising technique. What are they doing well? Would you be able to actualize something comparable?

Take as much time as is needed with titles – While we're regarding the matter, Upworthy is well known for their executioner, interactive features. Indeed, even a brilliant blog entry won't get the consideration it merits without a decent title. Would it be a good idea for it to be shrewd? Eye-getting? Website optimization amicable? Consider what will engage your gathering of people. It's suggested you compose upwards of 5-10 titles for each article, at that point pick the best!

4-1-1 – The 4-1-1 idea originates from Andrew Davis, creator of Brandscaping. Davis' web based life sharing procedure manages that for each six bits of substance shared via web-based networking media:

4 ought to be content from other industry influencers that is significant to your gathering of people

1 ought to be your own unique, instructive substance

1 ought to have a business viewpoint (coupon, item news, public statement), otherwise known as, a bit of substance the vast majority will essentially overlook.

The reasoning behind the 4-1-1 idea is that when you share industry thought administration, you're building connections inside the business and exhibiting a specific dimension of benevolence which procures genuine notoriety focuses that prove to be useful in the whole deal.

Innovative Marketing Ideas [Summary]

Prepared to develop your business? Experiment with these 64 imaginative advertising thoughts:

1. Advance your online networking handles, even face to face
2. Participate on famous hashtags
3. Make short, captivating Vine recordings
4. Stick your site pictures and illustrations on Pinterest
5. Monitor contenders' social profiles
6. Attempt urban advertising like flyers, publications, and walkway chalk
7. Commission a painting
8. Utilize your surroundings further bolstering your good fortune
9. Think about surprising sponsorships
10. Host a photograph challenge
11. Host a video challenge
12. Host a casting a ballot challenge
13. Host a subtitle challenge
14. Host a decent out-dated sweepstakes
15. Post to bargain destinations like Groupon
16. Add a hashtag to your challenges
17. Make challenges too sharable via web-based networking media
18. Offer extra focuses for sharing challenges
19. Inform email supporters of challenges
20. Advance your challenge on (every) social medium

21. Compose content took into account your gathering of people
22. Add a visual component to ALL your substance pieces
23. Make information stuffed infographics
24. Use layouts to make content creation less demanding
25. Incorporate diagrams and graphs in your substance
26. Use recordings for intuitiveness
27. Influence the intensity of records
28. Make intense future expectations
29. Infuse debate into your duplicate
30. Total amazing substance from different sources
31. Make an "ask the specialists" roundup
32. Compose applicable best 10 records
33. Furthermore, different records, as well!
34. Compose an item examination direct
35. Connection to your current substance with CTAs
36. Post introductions on Slideshare
37. Host free online classes
38. Get thoughts from Google related inquiry
39. Go through pop select ins on presentation pages
40. Use examination to exploit well known substance
41. Compose eBooks
42. Make 101 advisers for show the nuts and bolts

43. Advance your substance
44. Post about industry hotly debated issues
45. Compose (and permit) visitor posts
46. Make white papers
47. Just create quality substance
48. Give your organization some identity and don't be reluctant to utilize it
49. Add to online magazines
50. Host a digital broadcast
51. Spread neighborhood and news related occasions
52. Team up with companions
53. Make viral images
54. Utilize social verification in your substance
55. Divvy up your substance
56. Direct a substance review
57. Make marked instruments
58. Make and advance versatile explicit substance
59. Use gamification to advance association
60. Find and offer substance by others
61. Make entertaining web funnies
62. Duplicate the bosses
63. Take as much time as is needed with substance titles
64. Stick to Andrew Davis' 4-1-1 content technique

25 Marketing Tips That Will Revive Your Small Business Marketing Efforts

When you work all day every day on promoting plans and showcasing methodologies you can wind up in a drought with an absence of new thoughts. This can be a disappointing position to be in. I've discovered that when I hit an inventive drought it invests energy checking on promoting tips and thoughts. By doing this, it frequently gives a shock to my innovative reasoning and I push through the advertising mind hindrance.

Browsing advertising tips and thoughts or notwithstanding scanning for them online can be a tedious errand so today I'm going to impart to you 25 promoting tips that I generally discover take me from adhered to profitable inside a brief period time. Maybe these thoughts will work for you also.

General Marketing Tips and Ideas

Take an interest in LinkedIn Groups that are about your industry. Utilize those gatherings to pick up knowledge to what your clients are searching for and what your rivals are doing.

Remember the 80/20 rule, 80% of your business will originate from 20% of your clients. Is it accurate to say that you are remarketing to your present or past clients? If not, today could be a decent day to begin.

Request referrals. Referrals can help in developing your business and a great many people will confide in their companions, family and partners over a showcasing message or ad. Why not request referrals.

Measure your promoting, realize what works and what doesn't and clearly invest more energy in the endeavors that get your outcomes. What battle presented to you the most outcomes and have you taken a stab at accomplishing something like it of late? Your answer could be directly before you.

At the point when stuck take a seat with a scratch pad or thought diary. Simply begin composing - you'll be flabbergasted and what you can think of by simply giving your mind a chance to ponder and scribbling down your thoughts.

Item Marketing Tips:

Know your market. On the off chance that you are pitching to a B2C crowd center around the highlights, in the event that you are pitching to a B2B showcase concentrating on the advantages is the best approach. B2C is about how you affect them. B2B is about how you spare them time and cash.

Utilize social destinations like Pinterest and Instagram to grandstand photographs of your items. Ensure the photographs are great quality and truly demonstrate the craftsmanship of your item.

Item tributes can help you in getting shoppers keen on buying your item. Your tributes don't generally need to be composed, what about use video innovation and truly include a significant proclamation. The video is likewise incredible for displaying a showing.

Assess your promoting channels. It is safe to say that they are contacting your target group? Are there different channels you could attempt? Consider it, on the off chance that you are showcasing to youthful moms you will discover them in altogether different spots than you would 50-year-elderly people men. Why not conceptualize and investigate some new channels?

Is it accurate to say that you are gathering audits and evaluations on your item? Surveys assume a major job with purchasers with regards to basic leadership.

Administration Marketing Tips

Investigate your promoting message, how are you contending? Administration organizations will in general observe incredible outcomes when their showcasing message is outfitted towards the esteem that they give.

Do you give administrations to private clients? Feel free to take a stab at utilizing an impetus for them out you an attempt. You can target explicit postal divisions and market utilizing an administration like Groupon or ValPak.

There is no such thing as "one and done" with regards to promoting your administration business. Keep in contact with clients on a reliable premise to guarantee that they consider you when they need your administration once more.

Position your business as a specialist in your industry. Expound on your industry, talk, eat and learns. Get out there with the goal that when customers need your administration, they consider you.

Lead Q&A webcasts welcoming shoppers to go along with you and make inquiries. Google+ Hangouts makes this simple.

On the web and Digital Marketing Tips

You don't need to be on each informal community, however complete a kick-ass work on the ones you are on.

Ensure your site extends the demonstrable skill and the message that is a genuine portrayal of your business. Goodness, and keeping in mind that you are evaluating your site make sure and reach structure works. You'd be astounded at what number of don't.

Utilize convincing and drawing in duplicate on the web. On the off chance that you can't remain to peruse your site what makes you figure others will need to?

Set up alarms with the goal that you know when buyers are discussing you or searching for your item or administration. I use Google Alerts and Social Mention for social alarms.

Compose, compose and keep in touch with some more. Content is turning into a gigantic segment in web based advertising. On the off chance that you aren't an essayist, discover somebody that is.

Content Marketing Tips

Be steady. That will be key in your substance promoting achievement.

Content isn't simply message. Content incorporates can incorporate photographs, designs, video, and content. Be imaginative.

Try not to pass judgment on the achievement measurements of your substance until you've gone through a year building content. Results won't come speedy, however when they begin there will be no preventing the speculation from claiming time is justified, despite all the trouble.

Compose as though you are having a discussion, you aren't composing a research project and you need individuals to peruse it.

Invest the greater part of your energy in evergreen substance, or substance that will in any case be important in one, two and even five years.

18 Ways to Revive a Failed Product or Service

You likely recall a couple of well known item disappointments from similarly celebrated organizations. Google Glass, the New Coke, and the Ford Edsel ring a bell. However there are numerous renowned items that flopped yet later succeeded that don't really ring a bell.

Air pocket Wrap was made in 1957 as an in vogue backdrop. Truly. That item bombed so they attempted to showcase it as protection for nurseries and homes. That was better, yet it wasn't until IBM utilized Bubble Wrap to secure PC shipments that the item succeeded. At that point there's James Dyson, who starts creating and constructing 5,127 models of his acclaimed vacuum cleaner in 1979. In 1995, after dismissal by all the real makers, it at last turns into a top rated item in the UK.

These accounts of effective items that fizzled at first ought to effortlessly motivate us to take stock when looked with an item disappointment. Try not to devastate that extraordinary thought... at this time. It is in fact conceivable to re-dispatch a fizzled item or resuscitate a diminishing item. Also, if your business impulses are typically right, that is significantly more motivation to make sense of what turned out badly.

Break down Why Your Product or Service Failed or Why It's Dying

In one sense, no item is ever a total disappointment in the event that you get familiar with the exercises concerning why it fizzled. Information examination about the disappointment can tremendously enhance your client involvement with different items.

In How to Recover from a Failed Product Launch, Kissmetrics proposes the initial step is to break down the entirety of your measurements about the item dispatch itself. On the off chance that you use Google Analytics, that is a decent spot to begin. You can likewise get great knowledge from your contact the board framework and email stage. Gather information anyplace you can.

From that point onward, converse with and review your clients and target market to get input on the item. On the off chance that you use merchants, converse with them, as well. Once more, gather your item information anyplace and all over the place.

In the event that your examination persuades despite everything you have a feasible item, stage two is to redesign the item or potentially the showcasing. That is the place the diligent work starts. It takes a great deal of conceptualizing, mystery, and testing.

In view of that, here are 18 thoughts regarding how to renew a fizzled or blurring item.

1 - Give your item a name.

A name transforms an item into a brand and a brand has esteem. It suggests ability. It transforms the item into something that you, your customers, and your representatives can relate to.

Take a straightforward screwdriver set, for instance. What's all the more fascinating, a "Screwdriver Set" or "Pad Grip Screwdriver Set from Klein Tools?"

On the off chance that your organization is a perceived brand, or you possess a perceived brand name, use it. A "Specialist Screwdriver Set" from Sears has for quite a long time suggested polished methodology, quality, and lifetime execution.

Naming, a segment of marking, is a standout amongst the best approaches to resuscitate a fizzled item.

2 - Give it another name.

On the off chance that the item had a name the first run through around, attempt another one.

3 - Promote it utilizing media you didn't utilize the first run through around.

An excessive number of organizations limit their advertising message by adhering to what's typical in their industry, or by following what the other person is doing.

Obviously, your advertising should begin by characterizing your optimal customer(s) in incredible detail. At that point you discover where they can be achieved, where they hang out. Finally you utilize the media that will contact them.

I've seen organizations who, for example, just publicize on Facebook, or just in the paper, or just through a couple of other media. There is an immense range of media accessible through which you can pass on your item message. A short examining:

1. Magazines (print and computerized)
2. Online journals
3. Papers
4. Radio
5. TV
6. Neighborhood Events
7. Web based life (Facebook, LinkedIn, Twitter, Instagram, Pinterest, and then some)
8. Regular postal mail
9. Public expos
10. Business Networking
11. Exchange Associations

Truly, it's a ton of work. You additionally should make sure you can follow every one of your endeavors in every medium, so you know your Return on Investment, or Return on Marketing Dollars. The result is justified, despite all the trouble.

4 - Change the item informing.

Maybe your item takes care of a genuine issue, a genuine client torment point, yet you're not passing on it. The client doesn't see it.

5 - Change the item deals technique.

change your item deals technique

On the off chance that your item is sold through direct salesmen, there could be an imperfection in your item deals procedure or a missing ability with the sales rep. A few signs that your business methodology may require refreshing or that you may need to broaden the business procedure:

• Your prospects still have the torment point your item can unravel. This returns to informing.

• Your prospect never said "No." Most individuals are extremely occupied at work and it's anything but difficult to get derailed. In the event that you surrendered following a half year, you may need to stretch out the business cycle to twelve.

• Your sales rep just had contact with one individual in the organization. Numerous organizations, even little ones, have more than one individual associated with buy endorsements. You may talk a supervisor or managerial individual, yet the proprietor composes the check once the person in question is persuaded of the need.

6 - Tell an anecdote about your item.

Take a gander at your client socioeconomics. Who are they? What age? What are their side interests and interests? Pay? Discover all that you can and compose another tale about your item that interests to that fragment. Or then again compose different stories to speak to every statistic section.

For example, when I sold items to the print completing industry, I enclosed the item by numerous "accounts" to speak to my prospects job in the association. A story from my very own history about such a large number of additional time evenings and ends of the week and demolished occasions spoke to the end-client on the processing plant floor. With our item they could stay away from the surprising extra minutes situation, still complete all their work, and appreciate a long weekend with their family. For chiefs I had stories and tributes about decreased client grievance and smoother creation with less exertion. For organization proprietors, I had stories (contextual analyses) enumerating their potential quantifiable profit, customer procurement, and customer maintenance.

Your client doesn't really relate to your item. Be that as it may, they DO relate to human battles that are like their own. That is the place your story comes in to play.

7 - Get another person to advance your item.

Discover a non-contender who benefits your objective market and check whether they'd be keen on adding it to their product offering.

8 - Find another item dissemination channel.

Regardless of whether you're moving direct or moving through a solitary circulation channel, consider including another wholesaler channel. Alternately, in the event that you just move through circulation channels, consider moving straightforwardly. Today, offering items direct is anything but difficult to do with the accessibility of online video, online courses, telephone calls, and robotized contact the executives frameworks.

9 - Offer your item to beta test clients at a rebate, or for nothing.

Utilize the input to enhance the item and get tributes.

10 - Do an item dispatch.

Dispatches make fervor and buzz that creates much a larger number of leads than an exhausting old item discharge.

On the off chance that you completed an item dispatch the first run through around, do your item dispatch investigation as we talked about above, re-vamp it and the item if necessary, and attempt another dispatch.

11 - Speak at occasions gone to by your optimal clients.

Public exhibitions, nearby business organizing gatherings, and instructing bunches all need speakers.

12 - Host an occasion that likewise includes your item.

You could create an instructive occasion that enables your objective to advertise take care of a particular issue. You could likewise co-have it with other non-aggressive vital accomplices.

For instance, on the off chance that you pitch a unique doohickey to auto fix shops, you could hold an occasion that instructs nearby auto fix shops how to fix more vehicles every day without procuring additional staff. Obviously, it would incorporate your thingamajig.

13 - Target an alternate market.

Examine your item's optimal client. Perhaps you focused on the wrong individual. The Bubble Wrap story is the ideal case of how to discover diverse markets for your items.

14 - Change your item valuing.

In the event that it's a vast item with a few segments or administrations, break it separated into discrete items. It's conceivable your optimal client doesn't require all that you offer, yet would cheerfully purchase the segments.

Alternately, attempt packaged evaluating in which you include other profitable, related items or administrations, for the most part offering a markdown for the group. Once in a while the expansion of administrations, for example, free technical support, maintenace contracts, or service agreements can help slacking item deals, particularly with unpredictable, specialized items.

15 - Get vital showcasing counsel from a business mentor or advertising consultant.

My proposal is to do this progression regardless. When we're excessively near the activity in our organizations, it's difficult to reevaluate and split away in new ways, regardless of whether a group is included. An outside counsel with a new point of view and no contending plans can rapidly observe things you and your group may miss.

16 - Examine the social foundation of your item target markets.

In Cashing in on Culture: Breathing New Life into Old Brands, the creator advises us that culture can represent the moment of truth an item. Dr. Inka Crosswaite expresses, "numerous South Africans think lager in green jugs is 'posher' than brew in darker jugs, while the Greeks consider the classification the a different way."

We live in a multi-social world. We normally convey our social impacts and predispositions to those items and administrations we make. That is decisively why it's essential to inquire as to whether these impacts draw in or repulse our objective market, particularly on the off chance that we are moving globally.

17 - Get inventive, nearly to the point of insanity.

18 - Try an alternate visual search for your bundling and advancement.

Looks matter. On the off chance that conceivable, test a few plans. Not at all like years back, you don't need to spend much at all to get a lot of marvelous hand craft thoughts.

99designs is an intriguing method to get input from many creators, as appeared in the picture above, without employing them. You post a task ("challenge") and creators from around the globe present their fundamental plans for your item bundling. At the point when the challenge closes, you pick just the plan you like. The triumphant fashioner then completes the undertaking agreeable to you. In the impossible occasion that none of the plans bid to you, you don't need to pick a champ or pay for any of the entries.

I trust these 18 item recovery systems give you some significant takeaways.

Conclusion

Although the word brand in more the context of the consumer is limited to any company who is responsive, the word brand actually symbolizes any company that over time and regardless of the hour of day can be responsive with high standards of response. Brands will always go the extra mile for the customer. Marketing lost its way sometime back due to several factors including the need of business owner to start expecting marketing to bring in company revenue or profits.

I won't say that marketing cant be a profit making department of any company but the company needs to invest their time and money to enable it to do so.

There are two quotes that I firmly believe in,
"Our job is to connect to people, to interact with them in a way that leaves them better than we found them, more able to get where they'd like to go." – Seth Godin

"Make your marketing so useful people would pay you for it." – Jay Baer

So leaving you with these thoughts. Hope to be able to share my thoughts. Up until my next book.

www.ingramcontent.com/pod-product-compliance
Lightning Source LLC
Chambersburg PA
CBHW072223170526
45158CB00002BA/723